ACTS

AND

RESOLUTIONS

OF THE

NATIONAL COUNCIL

OF THE

MUSKOGEE NATION

OF

1893.

English and Creek.

Compiled by W. A. RENTIE.

SR Scholarly Resources Inc.
1508 Pennsylvania Avenue · Wilmington, Delaware 19806

SCHOLARLY RESOURCES, INC.
Wilmington, Delaware • London

Reprint edition published in 1975

Library of Congress Catalog Card Number: 75-3696
ISBN: 0-8420-1887-5

Manufactured in the United States of America

ACTS

AND

RESOLUTIONS

OF THE

NATIONAL COUNCIL

OF THE

MUSKOGEE NATION

OF

1893.

English and Creek.

Compiled by W. A. RENTIE.

MUSKOGEE, IND. TER.,
THE PHOENIX PRINTING COMPANY,
1894.

ACTS

AND

RESOLUTIONS

OF THE

NATIONAL COUNCIL

OF THE

MUSKOGEE NATION

OF

1893.

Compiled by W. A. RENTIE.

MUSKOGEE, IND. TER.,
THE PHOENIX PRINTING COMPANY,
1894.

AN ACT AUTHORIZING THE PRINTING OF THE ACTS AND RESOLUTIONS.

SECTION 1. The Principal Chief is hereby authorized and directed to appoint some competent person to compile all the laws passed by the present session of Council and have the same translated correctly into Creek and have them printed in one volume in pamphlet form.

SEC. 2. The work of compiling, translating and printing shall be done as soon after the adjournment of the present session of Council as possible. There shall be a thousand copies printed and one sent to each officer and member of Council and the balance shall be equally distributed to the several towns.

SEC. 3. For the purpose of carrying this act into effect there is hereby appropriated the sum of five hundred dollars ($500), or so much thereof as shall be necessary; and the Principal Chief shall report to Council the manner of the disbursement of the said amount.

SEC. 4. The needed corrections pointed out by the special committee appointed to examine the new compilation of the laws shall be included in the compilation and translation herein provided for.

Approved November 6, 1893.

L. C. PERRYMAN, Principal Chief.

INDEX.

ACTS OF CREEK COUNCIL--1893.

GAME LAW.

SECTION 1. Should any citizen of this Nation be found hunting game in this Nation in company with any United States citizen, he shall be liable to a fine of not less than one hundred dollars ($100).

SEC. 2. The prosecuting attorneys of the several districts shall prosecute all citizens violating this law.

Became a law by limitation, 1891.

LAWFUL FARM FENCE.

SECTION 1. A lawful rail fence shall be seven rails high, well staked and double-ridered.

SEC. 2. A straight fence, built of six rails or poles, whether fastened to posts with wire or nails, with two strands of wire stretched above the rails, shall be deemed a lawful fence.

SEC. 3. A lawful wire fence shall be of eight wires attached to posts eight feet apart and one stay between each two posts. The bottom wire shall be four inches above the ground, the second three inches above the first, the third four inches above the second, the fourth six inches above the third, the fifth seven inches above the fourth, the sixth eight inches above the fifth, the seventh twelve inches above the sixth, and the eighth fourteen inches above the seventh. The height shall be four feet and ten inches, with strong corner posts well braced.

SEC. 4. When any citizen shall have a lawful fence as defined in this act, and the stock or property of another citizen shall damage or injure his crops, he shall be entitled to damages for such injury, which shall be assessed by two disinterested persons, said persons to be appointed by the judge of the district wherein said damage is done.

SEC. 5. No citizen not having a lawful fence shall be entitled to damages done to his crops by the stock of another.

Approved October 11, 1893.

PROHIBITING THE LEASING OF LAND.

SECTION 1. It shall be unlawful for any citizen of this Nation to lease for a term of years any portion of the unoccupied domain to any non-citizen to be occupied or improved by the non-citizen at his own expense in consideration of his occupancy and use of said land for said term of years.

SEC. 2. If any person shall violate this law he shall, upon conviction before the District Court, forfeit all such improvement to the Nation and be liable to a fine of one hundred dollars ($100).

Approved November 6, 1893.

AMENDMENT TO TIMBER LAW.

Section 400 of the timber law found on page 133 of the law book, edition 1893, shall not be so construed as to invest any person with the personal right or title to timber or land within the half mile limit therein mentioned, but the same shall be public domain for all purposes other than for making railroad ties as provided for in the said act.

Approved October 24, 1893.

AMENDMENT TO WALNUT TIMBER LAW.

SECTION 1. The act of the National Council, approved October, 1889, found on page 60 of law book, edition 1890, authorizing Snow Sells to take charge of and dispose of all down walnut timber, is hereby repealed.

SEC. 2. Section 155 of the law found on page 60 of the law book, edition 1893, prohibiting the selling of walnut timber and fixing a penalty for violation of the same, is hereby so amended that any person failing to pay the fine therein provided for shall receive fifty lashes on the bare back for each and every offense, and if any officer shall be found guilty of a violation of this act he shall, upon conviction before the court, be removed from office in addition to the payment of said fine.

Approved October 24, 1893.

GRADING THE PRIMARY SCHOOLS.

After the 30th of May, 1894, the following law shall be in force:

SECTION 1. There shall be three grades of Primary Schools, namely: First, Second and Third.

SEC. 2. There shall be fifteen of the first grade, to

average twenty in attendance; twenty-five of the second grade, to average fifteen; and twenty-five of the third grade, to average ten.

SEC. 3. Teachers of the first grade shall receive $35.00 per month; of the second grade $30.00 per month; of the third grade $25.00 per month.

SEC. 4. The teachers shall be given graded certificates, and appointed to schools accordingly.

SEC. 5. The Board of Education is hereby authorized to make such rules and regulations as will best facilitate the grading and appointing of schools and teachers.

Approved October 19, 1893.

RELATING TO BOARDING SCHOOLS.

SECTION 1. The superintendents of the intermediate and high schools shall be nominated by the Chief and confirmed by Council. They must be persons of good moral character and competency, and shall be liable to impeachment.

SEC. 2. The superintendent of any intermediate or high school shall be responsible for any indebtedness he may incur for his school, which may exceed the regular appropriation for said school.

SEC. 3. He shall take his position upon the 5th of December next following his election and shall hold his office for the term of two years.

SEC. 4. He shall have a right, with the approval of the trustees, to select the teachers and employees for his school, the teachers to hold certificates from the board, and may discharge any teacher or employee for incompetency or immoral conduct, and replace same with the approval of the trustees.

Sec. 5. The salary of superintendent of schools accommodating 100 pupils shall be $700.00; of schools accommodating 50 pupils, $500.00; of the Creek Orphan Asylum, $700.00; of the Colored Orphan Asylum, $500.00 per annum, to be paid quarterly as to other standing officers.

Sec. 6. The books for the intermediate and high schools shall be paid for out of the regular appropriation for their respective schools.

Sec. 7. The members of the board shall be liable to impeachment.

Sec. 8. The Chief shall have power to suspend any member of the board or any superintendent upon sufficient charges being made, and may appoint a substitute to hold the office until the following Council.

Sec. 9. The board shall not accept the report of superintendent when vouchers do not accompany, and shall issue no order for warrant until proper report is made, and if the board issue such order without proper vouchers the members of the board shall be responsible to that amount.

Sec. 10. This law shall not be so construed as to deprive any superintendent now in office of his position, but shall confirm his appointment for the ensuing year.

Sec. 11. From and after the passage of this act it shall be in full force and virtue.

Approved November 1, 1893.

RELATING TO ORPHANS AT ASYLUMS.

Section 1. Any orphan may be admitted into an asylum at any age over eight and under eighteen years, and shall be compelled to remain there under the authority of the superintendent until they shall have attained the age of twenty-one years, unless continued sickness or improper conduct compels them to leave.

Provided, however, That any orphan over twelve years old who may have business at home requiring their attention shall be allowed to return home during the vacation, and *provided*, that if any orphan who is in an asylum has a guardian who wishes to enter said orphan in a higher school, such guardian shall have the right to do so.

SEC. 2. The trustees of the asylums shall be required to keep the asylum full according to law having in view the appropriation for same.

Approved November 6, 1893.

TO DISSOLVE CONTRACT CONCERNING NUYAKA MISSION.

Be it resolved by the National Council of the Muskogee Nation, That the Board of Education be and is hereby instructed and directed to give notice of a disolution of the contract of 1893 with the Presbyterian Board of Home Missions regarding Nuyaka Mission, which dissolution shall take place upon the end of the present school term of the said school.

Approved November 1, 1893.

AMENDMENT TO LAW PROVIDING FOR LIVE STOCK INSPECTOR.

SECTION 1. The term of office of the live stock inspector shall be two years.

SEC. 2. He shall be elected by Council.

SEC. 3. He shall file a bond with the National Treasurer in the sum of twenty thousand dollars ($20,000). He shall report to the National Council annually all monies accruing under his office.

Approved October 19, 1893.

AMENDMENT TO LICENSE LAW.

The license tax law is hereby so amended as to include the following taxes:

Sewing Machine Co., per year,	$25.00
Auctioneers in house or tent, per day,	3.00
Auctioneers on street, per day,	2.00
Dime shows, per week,	1.00

Approved October 27, 1893.

DEW M. WISDOM, U. S. Indian Agent.
L. C. PERRYMAN, Principal Chief M. N.

PROHIBITING NON-CITIZENS FROM GATHERING PECANS.

The Principal Chief of the Muskogee Nation is hereby authorized and directed to request the United States Indian Agent to prohibit all non-citizens from gathering and selling pecans from off the public domain.

Approved October 25, 1893.

REGARDING INDIGENTS.

The resolution defining who are indigents and entitled

to money from the Nation as such, shall be so amended as to read, "No person drawing money as pension from the United States government shall be entitled to any money from this Nation under the head of indigent."

Approved October 19, 1893.

PROHIBITING JUDGES FROM EMPLOYING ASSISTANT LIGHT HORSEMEN.

From and after the passage of this act no District Judge shall have the right to employ or use any assistant Light Horsemen; and if any Judge shall violate this law he shall be immediately suspended from office by the Principal Chief; and if any person shall serve as assistant Light Horseman under appointment from any Judge he shall not be paid by the Nation.

Approved November 6, 1893.

REGARDING RAILROADS.

In the event of the election of a delegation to represent the interests of this Nation at Washington, they are hereby authorized and directed to earnestly urge the proper authorities of the United States to repeal so much of the acts of Congress approved respectively July 25, 26 and 27, 1866, authorizing the construction of certain railroads through the Indian Territory, and as grants to such railroad companies, giving each alternate section of land of our present domain for twenty miles on each side of such railroads.

Approved November 6, 1893.

REGARDING ELECTION OF PRINCIPAL CHIEF.

From and after the 5th of December, 1891, no person shall be entitled to any election to the office of Principal Chief, who, at an election lawfully held, shall not have received a majority of all the votes cast as contemplated by a strict construction of the letter of the Constitution bearing upon the subject of the election of the Principal Chief.

Became a law by limitation, 1891.

PROHIBITING CLERKS OF COURTS FROM PRACTICING LAW IN THEIR COURTS.

No Judge of any of the Courts of this Nation shall allow the clerk of his Court to practice law before his Court; and for a violation of this act he shall be subject to removal from office.

Approved October 26, 1893.

PROVIDING FOR ATTORNEY-GENERAL FOR THE NATION.

A competent attorney at law, well versed in the laws of the Creek Nation and conversant with both the English and Creek languages, shall be elected by the National Council at its present session, whose duty shall be to institute suit or suits before the Supreme Court against any person or officer, owing the Nation any sum of money for any purpose or on any account whatever, and to prosecute such cases vigorously and have the same commenced before the next June term of the Supreme Court. The said attorney shall file a bond of ten thousand dollars ($10,000.00) before the Principal Chief, conditioned upon the faithful discharge of his duties as such attorney. The said attorney shall have the authority to direct the the Judges of the several Districts to execute his orders and the judgments of the Supreme Court, and if any judgment be rendered against any person or officer in default with the Nation and a collection of the judgment is attempted, the exemption law as appears in Chapter XIII, pages 90 and 91, Edition, 1893, shall not be construed so as to operate against the collection of said judgment. The said attorney shall be allowed his actual traveling expenses and boarding expenses and also 25 per cent. of all monies secured by him for the Nation, and turned into the National Treasury. The said attorney shall serve for two years from the 5th of December, 1893. He shall make annual report to the National Council.

Approved November 3, 1893.

PROVIDING FOR THREE COMMISSIONERS FOR THE NATION.

SECTION 1. There is hereby created a commission to be composed of three competent persons to be elected by the National Council and to continue in office from their election to the annual session of Council of 1894. They shall visit every non-citizen residing in this Nation and register the names of each member of each family, their race or color, and an inventory of all live stock, held or claimed by them. They shall ascertain as near as may be, without an actual survey thereof, the number of acres of all lands enclosed for farms, pastures, orchards, gardens, town or other lots, together with all other improvements such as houses, barns or sheds occupied, held or owned by them; the particular occupation of each and the authority under which each claim to own, occupy or enjoy the properties herein mentioned. They shall also ascertain the origin, nature and character of any right, title or privileges claimed in or to such live stock, farm, pasture or other improvement and render a full report in detail to the next regular session of the National Council.

SEC. 2. In order to more effectually carry into operation the provisions of this act, the United States Indian Agent of the Union Agency is hereby requested to detail one of his policeman to accompany each commissioner, if he shall need one, to aid in serving any summons he may find necessary to issue for the appearance of persons needed in making the investigations herein provided for; each commissioner shall also, in cases of actual necessity have the right to the services of the Light Horse Company of the District wherein he may be at work, and the District Judges are hereby instructed to honor any requisition made by him for such service in the legal discharge of such duties herein imposed upon him.

SEC. 3. If the commissioners shall find any non-citizen residing in this country contrary to the Treaties, the United States statutes or the laws of this country, they shall report the same to the Indian Agent and request his removal from the country, and if for any cause the Agent shall fail either to act, or cause his removal within a reasonable time, the commissioner shall then report the matter to the Interior Department and ask his removal.

SEC. 4. That portion of the law requiring district solicitors to report intruders to the Indian Agent is hereby repealed, *provided*, that nothing herein contained shall be construed so as to interfere with the additional one hundred dollars ($100.00) per annum allowed solicitors by said law.

SEC. 5. The pay of each commissioner is hereby fixed at three dollars ($3.00) per day, and that of the policeman at one dollar ($1.00) per day, provided that no greater amount in the aggregate than one thousand dollars ($1000.00) shall be paid to any commissioner and his assistant during his term of office.

Approved November 3, 1893.

RESOLUTION TO BE PRESENTED TO THE UNITED STATES COMMISSIONERS.

SECTION 1. It is the sense of this body that any change in the present status of the Indian Territory that would include the Muskogee Nation within the limits of an organized State of the American Union, would be contrary to the best interests of the citizens of the Nation, and any proposition of Congress to effect such a change or to include this Nation in any State or Territory wherein the present Territory of Oklahoma shall be a component part is greatly to be deprecated and resisted by all proper means.

SEC. 2. The Principal Chief is hereby instructed to furnish copies of these resolutions to any commission or committee that may be sent out to visit this Territory under act of the last regular session of Congress, to the Secretary of the Interior and to the United States Indian Agent at Muskogee.

Approved November 1, 1893.

APPROPRIATING $600,000 TO BE PAID PER CAPITA.

SECTION 1. $600,000 of the money, $2,000,000, derived from the sale of the Oklahoma lands and now standing to the credit of the Muskogee Nation with the United States Government, shall be withdrawn and be distributed per capita to the citizens of the Muskogee Nation.

SEC. 2. The National Council now in session shall immediately proceed to enact legislation to make this act effective.

Approved October 24, 1893.

REQUISITION UPON THE UNITED STATES FOR THE $600,000.

The Principal Chief is hereby authorized and directed, for and on behalf of the Muskogee Nation, to make requisition upon the proper authorities of the United States in such forms as may be necessary or required by the said authorities for the payment to the National Treasurer of the Muskogee Nation, of the sum of $600,000, out of the amount of money in the Treasury of the United States to the credit of the Muskogee Nation on account of the sale to the United States, under act of cession and agreement entered into January 19, 1889, of the lands ceded to the United States under treaty, 1866. Such requisition when made shall be taken and accepted and is hereby declared to be the requisition of the proper authorities of the Muskogee Nation.

Approved November 4, 1893.

EMPLOYMENT OF GEN. COLBY AS ATTORNEY FOR THE NATION AT WASHINGTON, D. C.

SECTION 1. Hon. Leonard W. Colby, an attorney of

long standing, of Washington, D. C., is hereby employed as attorney for the Muskogee Nation to defend the interests of the Muskogee Nation in all suits pending or that may hereafter be brought in the Court of Claims or the Supreme Court of the United States for Indian depredations, for the term of three years, at an annual salary of four thousand dollars ($4,000.00.)

SEC. 2. The Principal Chief of the Muskogee Nation is hereby authorized and directed to enter into a written contract with said attorney on behalf of said Nation for such employment.

SEC. 3. There is hereby appropriated an amount for the payment of said salary and the Principal Chief is authorized to issue warrants therefor and the National Treasurer to pay the same from the funds of the National Treasury as provided by law.

Approved November 6, 1893.

RESOLUTION TO HAVE BOUNDARY LINE BETWEEN EUFAULA AND MUSKOGEE DISTRICTS SURVEYED.

The Principal Chief is hereby authorized and directed to appoint two disinterested persons, not residents of either Eufaula or Muskogee Districts to go to the boundary line between the two Districts and beginning at Hopoethle Yoholar's cow pen run the line to Soda Springs, defining same by posts or stakes, and report to present Council.

Approved October 14, 1893.

ACT ADOPTING SURVEY AS REPORTED MADE BY CÆSAR ROGERS AND MARSEY HARJO.

The District boundary line between the Eufaula and Muskogee Districts, as traced and established by Cæsar Rogers and Marsey Harjo, so as to run 220 feet North of W. E. Gentry & Co's. store and 143 feet North of Fisher Mercantile Co's. store, is hereby accepted and declared to be the correct boundary between the said Districts; the said Rogers and Harjo being appointed surveyors under the above act.

Approved October 24, 1893.

PROVIDING FOR ATTACHMENT OF PROPERTY IN LITIGATION.

SECTION 1. From and after the passage of this act when a case has been instituted in any District Court or in the Supreme Court and the plaintiff has reason to believe that the property in dispute is about to be disposed of by sale or otherwise, or to be removed from the limits of this Nation for the purpose of defeating any judgment which may be rendered by the Court, he may apply to the Court for a writ of injunction restraining the defendant from disposing of such property.

SEC. 2. Before such injunction or attachment can issue, the plaintiff shall state under oath, with not less than two witnesses, that such property is about to be disposed of or removed, and also file a bond with not less than two responsible sureties in a sum twice the amount of property to be attached, for the payment of such damage or damages as may be sustained by the defendant in case the plaintiff fails to gain his suit.

SEC. 3. If any defendant in any cause shall dispose of any property by sale, removal from the country or otherwise after the same has been attached or enjoined by order of the Court, he shall be deemed guilty of larceny and shall be punished accordingly.

Approved November 6, 1893.

PROVIDING FOR A CONVENTION TO MAKE A NEW CONSTITUTION.

SECTION 1. All the male citizens of voting age of the several towns shall meet in their respective towns at the usual place of meeting on the 15th day of December, 1893, and shall then and there proceed to elect two delegates to represent their towns and the delegates thus elected shall meet at Okmulgee, M. N., on the first Tuesday in January, 1894, and then and there organize by electing a chairman from one of their number and a clerk and interpreter from outside.

SEC. 2. The said delegation, when thus organized, shall proceed to prepare and draft a new Constitution for the Muskogee Nation, which when completed shall be submitted to the Principal Chief.

SEC. 3. When the Principal Chief shall receive the proposed new Constitution he shall have the same carefully translated and printed in both English and Creek, and shall send a copy of each to every Town Chief, and shall also order the Town Chiefs to call a meeting of all voters in their respective towns and to submit to them the new Constitution for adoption or rejection by popular vote. The Town Chiefs shall call the voters of their towns to meet on the second Tuesday in June, 1894, to vote on said Constitution. The

Principal Chief shall furnish the necessary blanks and the votes shall be recorded in duplicate, one copy to be held by the Town Chief and the other to be forwarded to the President of the House of Kings, and the President of the House of Kings shall submit all such returns to the National Council at its regular session in October, 1894.

SEC. 4. If the Constitution, as herein above provided for, shall be ratified by a majority vote of the people, then the Principal Chief shall promulgate the same by proclamation and thereupon it shall become and be the Constitution of the Muskogee Nation, *provided, however*, that nothing therein contained shall be taken, construed or held to in any way interfere with the present Constitution and laws, or any officer now in office until after the expiration of the present Constitutional term of Council, *except, however*, that the next general election for the election of Principal Chief and Second Chief, and members of the Council shall be held in accordance with the new Constitution.

SEC. 5. The said delegates shall each receive two dollars ($2.00) per day while in attendance at the meeting and mileage at the rate of ten cents (10c.) per mile in going to and returning from the Capitol. The clerk and interpreter shall receive the same per diem and mileage as the delegates.

SEC. 6. The convention of delegates herein provided for, shall not sit longer than twenty days, exclusive of Sundays.

SEC. 7. For the purpose of carrying this act into effect there is hereby appropriated the sum of five thousand dollars ($5,000.00), or so much thereof as may be necessary.

Approved November 1, 1893.

APPENDIX.

Supreme Court Decisions.

RELATING TO ESTATES.

Hon. L. C. Perryman, Principal Chief, M. N.:

Dear Sir—Your communication relating to the law on page 94, Section 267, law book, edition 1893, which reads: "and a child's part if there be children," should either the husband or wife die and survivor also die before the estate is settled, would either the husband or wife who dies last be entitled to the heir's part?

The Court, after due consideration, is of the opinion that either the husband or wife dying last and before the estate is settled should be entitled to the heir's part, and it is so declared.

ISPARHECHER, Chief Justice, *pro tem.*

November 3, 1893.

RELATING TO MARRIAGE.

Hon. L. C. Perryman, Principal Chief, M. N.:

Yours, submitting to the Court and requesting the

Court's opinion and decision on law which reads: "and any marriage contracted in writing or in the presence of two or more witnesses who shall sign the marriage contract as such shall be lawful." The Court is of the opinion and decrees that no marriage is legal unless the contract is in writing and signed by two or more witnesses, and no marriage contract should be solemnized by any authorized officer or minister unless such contract is reduced to writing and properly signed, and it is so declared.

ISPARHECHER, Chief Justice, *pro tem.*

November 3, 1893.

CORRECTIONS OF LAWS, EDITION 1893, AS MADE BY EXAMINING COMMITTEE.

OMISSIONS.

Section 324 should read: "The Captain shall then post and advertise all estray stock reported to him for the period of six months, *giving due notice of time and place of sale*, and sell the same at public sale to the highest bidder for National warrants, scrip or cash."

To Section 329 should be added: "and shall pay one-third of the amount for which the same shall have been sold to the purchaser from whom he proves the stock."

To Section 115 should be added: "And the District Judge shall file a bond of two thousand dollars ($2,000.)"

EAST AND WEST RAILROAD.

Be it Resolved, That it is the opinion of the National

Council of the Muskogee Nation, that the construction, by a company duly authorized by Congress, of a branch railroad from a point on the eastern boundary of the Muskogee Nation, running westward to connect with the Missouri, Kansas & Texas railroad at some point between Muskogee and Eufaula, so as to form a continuous road, in conjunction with the main line, to our southern boundary, is in accordance with the stipulations of the Treaty of June 14, 1866, between the Muskogee Nation and the United States, which concedes the "right of way to any Company which shall be duly authorized by Congress, and shall, with the express consent of the Secretary of the Interior, undertake to construct a railroad from * * * * any point on their eastern to their southern or western boundary" as the same completes and exhausts all railroad grants and franchises conceded by existing Treaties between the United States and the Muskogee Nation; *provided, however*, that nothing herein shall be so construed as to infer any expression of opinion in regard to the question as to what company may be duly authorized by Congress.

Approved November 2, 1881.

SUPREME COURT DECISION.

OKMULGEE, Ind. Ter., October 22, 1881.

* * * * It is held by the Court that the Constitution makes the action or decision of this Court a finality. To reopen any case after a decision by this body would defeat the design of the Constitution. * * * *

D. N. McINTOSH, Chief Justice.

* * * * The testimony of any person whether re-

lated to the party in the suit or not, is admissible before any of the Courts of this Nation. * * * * Circumstantial evidence is to be admitted in any of the Courts of this Nation.

JAMES FIFE, Chief Justice.

CHANGES TO BE MADE.

In Chapter for adopted citizens, substitute the name of Thos. Hawkins for Lizzie Hawkins; Josephine Freeman for Josephine Bruner; and M. A. Rickets for M. O. Rickets.

Este Maskoke Tulwv-vlke Nakvfte

AHAKV MOMEN AKERRICKV HAYVTE,

OHKOLOPE,

1893.

W. A. RENTIE, Sanoricv.

COKV SANORICV EMAHAKV.

SET. 1. Tulwv-vlke Em-Mekko yekcetv enhecket os momen emacahnetv haket os, momat este momar' tetayen oh mellvres hiyome Tulwvvlke nakvfte ahakv hahicat omvlkvn etohkvhlet heren Este Maskoke emoponvkv etohtvlhucheet etempvlsen cokv-tvpekse hvmkosen esanorievren.

SET. 2. Tulwv-vlke awah he erentopvrv en helvpke estohmmomosen ahakv esanorihoce tetayet on omat momehoevres. Ahakv esanorat cukpe rakko hvmket omvres, momen cuko-atehkvlke atekat momen enwiketv etvt o estomis hvmkvlken ematothoyvres, momen erahoskat etvl' arahrvkv etemmomvlkosen oh hawvhhohares.

SET. 3. Heyv ahakv esayeciekv ohfveevn evtokonawv cukpe cahkepet fieket os, monkat orekot o estomis etetayecen omat mvn yamahkuehoevres, momen heyv evtokonawv estomet yvmahken omat Tulwv-vlke emmekkot hvtvm Tulwv-vlke nakaftof emeohkerkueevres.

SET. 4. Espoke ahakv esanorihoevte ocat kvmmette esarahkose aketeckv hahye matmvye esheevte atekat heyv ahakv esanoran apahoyvres.

Oh hakvsamis, Ehole, 6, 1893.

LEKVS PELMVN, Mekko.

ESHECETV.

PONVTTV EMAHAKV.

SET. 1. Tvsekvyv estomet pun tvsekvyv tokon eyvpvyet es fayet esaret omet oh faccen omat cvtokonawv cukpe humkat ($100.00) sen nacomekon feyihocet omares.

SET. 2. Momen heyv ahakv kacket o atekat ekvntvckv estomat afvn omen omat, mv ofv ahakv municv huerat afastet omares.

Oh hakvsvmkv sekon ahakv haket os.

TOHOPKE EMVHAKV.

Cvpofv emvtohopke heyv elecv makan acvkkvyen hahoyet on omat ahakv acvkkvyet omares:

SET. 1. Tofvlvhle kolvpake enhvlwet omet, heren esen cvkcvhet omet, onvpv oh wakkv hokkolet omvres.

SET. 2. Tohopke lvputket on omat, tofvlvhle epaket cokelle svrvhrvket, munkat cvto-fvkv esvyekcicvkvtet omet, munkat remetvtot o estomis sayekcicvkvtet omet, momen tofvllvhle epaket onvpvn cvto-fvkv hokkolet asenephoket on omat mvt ahakv acvkkayet omvres.

SET. 3. Cokelet estele ahopakv cenvpaken yekcvken cvkcvhhet omet heren en tekkeket ohmen, cokele hokkolat atekat emetenrvwv senhuervt cakhe vlket, hiyome etetahkof cvto-fvkv cenapaket asenepket omvres, momen hiyomet asenepket omvres, elecv awakkatet ekvnv onvppv ahopakocs ostet omvres, momen esahokkolatet enhvteceskv awakkan eremonvppv ahopakoce tutcenet omvres, momen esatutcenatet ahopakoce osten akawvpket omvres, momen esostatet ahopakoce epaken akawvpket omvres, momen escahkepatet ahopakoce kolvpaken akawvpket omvres, momen esepakatet ahopakoce cenvpaket akawvpket omvres, momen escolvpakatet ahopakoce palen hokkolohkaken akawvpket omvres, momen escenvpakatet ahopakoce palen ostohkaken akvwapket omvres, momen tohopke erespokof enhvlwe estele ahopakv osten ahopakoce palet hoyvnet omvres.

SET. 4. Tohopke ahakv aevkkvyen ocepesas afvn apuekvt ennoksen omat mv ekvntuckv fveceevt este hokkole akerrvkekon oh melliyen nake yamahke ocan enraheevkvres, momen estomoset ennoksen omat esfveken apuekv epocaset feket omvres.

SET. 5. Ahakv aevkkvyekon tohopken oce sasen apuekat ennoksen omat feketv enheckekot omvres.

SET. 6. Ahakv estomet heyv ahakvn vurvpet ocen omat muev ateken aslet os.

Oh hakvsamis, Otvwoskv-rakko, 11, 1893.

LEKVS PELMVN, Mekko.

EKVNV PVLKV ASEHKV.

SET. 1. Ekvn' tvoleme tvntvke liketayan pun tasekiat tasekiah tokon ohrolope anacomen esaheckvn etemfveciyet empalet omatet mv tasekiah tokatet eme enevtokonawvn esyamahket cukot ot tohopke omakis oh hahicet omen mome nake oh hahicat ekvnv oh likepe nake se enhayepvranan esvrvhkvn omen omat ahakv vurvpet omvres.

SET. 2. Estimet heyv ahakvn kacen ekvntuckv fveekv

cuko ehomvn oh faccen omat nake emvtothoke ocakat omvlkvt tvlwv-vlke enake haket omvres, momen oh hatvlakat cvtokonawv cukpe hvmken feket omvres.

Oh hakvsamis, Ehole 6, 1893.

LEKVS PELMVN, Mekko.

ETO EMVHAKV ESEMMAHERICKV.

Sᴇᴛ. 1. Eto ohfvcev ahakv hakvte cokv eslikat, emvhonkvtkv 133 ocat, hiyomet apvke haket os, mv ahakv akerkv nvrkvpv emacayece make ocat, emofv ekvnvtot eto tepakat mv este emet okekot os, momis nake mv omat este Maskoke en tvlemet omvres.

Oh hakvsamis, Otvwoskv-rakko, 24, 1893.

LEKVS PELMVN, Mekko.

AHAHWV EMVHAKV ESEMMAHERICKV.

Sᴇᴛ. 1. Otvwoskv-rakko, 1882, amof ahakv haye Snow Sells ahahwv tolkakat celayepare yekcetv emvte, ahakv, 1890, esahotophoyvte cokv eslikat ofv mvhonkvtkv 120 eslikat, elet os.

Sᴇᴛ. 2. Ahakv mocvsat ofv mvhonkvtkv 60, Eto Emahakv ocan, hiyomet esemaherickv haket os; Feketvn omekot fekekon omat pale cahkepen rokafhoyet omvres, momis este enwiketvt heyv ahakv kacet on omat feyihcat tvlket hvtvm enwiketvn ossihocet omvres.

Oh hakvsamis, Otvwoskv-rakko, 25, 1893.

LEKVS PELMNV, Mekko.

COKV HECKV LOPOCKE OHFVCCV.

Kehvsse netta 30, 1894, hoyanof heyvt ahakvt omvres:

SET. 1. Emvhakv lopocke emvrvhrvkv tutcenet omvres, Enhateceskv, Esahokkolv momet Esatutcena maketvt omvres.

SET. 2. Enhateceskv palen cahkepohkaket omvres, momet hopoetake pale hokkolat netta arahkv oren emahayet omvres; esahokkolat palen cahkepohkaket omvres, momet hopoetake netta arrahkv emahayat palen cahkepohkaket omvres; momen esatutcenat pale hokkolen cvhkepohkaket omvres, momet hopoetake palat netta arahkv oren emahayet omvres.

SET. 3. Enhateceskv mvhayvlke en feketv hvsse hvmkat cvtokonawv pale tutcenen cahkepohkaket omvres, esahokkolat hvsse arahkv pale tutcenet omvres, momen esatutcenat pale hokkolen cvhkepohkaket omvres.

SET. 4. Emvhakv cuko oh haketecvlke emvhayvlke cokv sem ossicat enkerretv acvkkvyen setenhvlhvwen sem ossicet omvres, momen cokv enheckat acvkkvye etan oh melhoyet omvres.

SET. 5. Emvhakv cuko oh haketecvlke yekcetv ocet ahakoce esen hayet heyv ahakv acvkkayen e sohfvccecet omvres.

Oh hakvsamis, Otvwoskv-rakko, 19, 1893.

LEKVS PELMVN, Mekko.

COKV HECKV CUKO RAKRAKAT OHFVCCV.

SET. 1. Cokv heckv cuko rakrakat oh hafastvlke Mekkot oh mellen Tvlwvvlket oh hetemaret enwiketv sapvklecet omvres; momen este ensehoketv heraket omvres momen en-cokv-kerretv momvr' heret omakvres, momen opunayecet enwiketv ossihoce tetayet omvres.

SET. 2. Cokv heckv cuko oh hafastvlke em mahakvcuko esiyecickv Tulwvvlke catokonawv enfiyecican eresemontvlen yamahkuecaket on omat eme mahosaten ahuerv enhakaket omvres.

SET. 3. Cokv heckv cuko oh hafastvlke enwiketv hahohye aye Rafo Rakko en netta 5, orof ematotketv erohsapvklvres, momen ohrolope hokkolen sapaklet omvres.

SET. 4. Cokv heckv cuko oh hafastvlke en cokv heckv cuko emahayaranat mvhayvlke palaket omvres, momen atotkvlke omis palaket omvres, momis mahakv cuko oh hecvlke emakvsaman talkosen palaket omvres, momis mvhayvlken palaken omat cokv heckv cuko oh hafastvlke cokv semossicvte talkosen palaket omvres; momen mvhayvlke tot munkat atotkvlket o estomis omvkekot omaket munkat ensehoketvt herakekot on omat essosicetv yekcetv ocvket omvres, momen essoscicen omat ayoposke ohmellaket omvres oh hecvlke asen kerren.

SET. 5. Cokv heckv cuko rakrakat hopoetake cukpe humke atehkat oh hafastvlke, momen Este Cate ecke melle emmvhakv cuko oh hafastv esyomat enfeketv ohrolope hvmkat cvtokonawv cukpe kolvpaket ($700.00) omvres, momen mvhakv cuko hopoetake pale cvhkepe atehkat momen Ena Lvste ecke mele em mvhakv cuko esyomat oh hafastvlke ohrolope hvmkat cukpe cahkepet enheckaket omvres, momen enwiketv etv cvtokonap escaekv semossihocat etvpomen sosset omvres.

SET. 6. Cokv heckv cuko rakrakat esayecickv catokonawv fiekan a ossen nak cokv esenneshoyet omvres.

Sᴇᴛ. 7. Cokv heckv cuko oh haketeevlke este tuteenat opunayeeet enwiketv sossihoce tetayet omvres.

Sᴇᴛ. 8. Cokv heckv cuko oh haketeevlke este tuteenat tot, munkat cokv heckv cuko rakrakat oh hafastvlket o estomis svnrvpkv momvr' tetayet enhaken omat Mekkot afekhonniceetv yekeetv oeet omvres, momen ayaposke ohmellet omvres tvlwvvlke en nakvftetv rateken.

Sᴇᴛ. 9. Cokv heckv cuko rakrakat oh hafastvlke eohkerkuecakat ayoposke cokv apakvkekon omaken omat oh hafastvlke este tuteenat e enakueevkekot omvres, momen evtokonap ecaehkv esheckueeskv cokv semossievkekot omvres, momen oh hafastvlke em meohkerkueckvt orekot omofvn oh haketeevlket evtokonap escaehkv es heckueckvn cokvn sem ossicaket on omat oh haketeevlke min ahuetv enhaket omvres.

Sᴇᴛ. 10. Heyv ahakv hakat cokv heckv cuko oh hafastvlk' hiyome sehokat enwiketv akonahet omekares. momis heyv ohrolope hvmke ayvranat emohyekeicet os.

Sᴇᴛ. 11. Heyv ahakv hoyanan apaken enyekee kawvpiket ayvres.

Oh hakvsamis, Ohole 1, 1893.

LEKVS PELMVN, Mekko.

ECKE-MELE COKV HECKV CUKO APOKAT OHFVCCV.

Sᴇᴛ. 1. Ecke-mele estomis emvculkv ohrolope cenvpakat asenkvnevpekot momen palen cenvpohkakat esenhoyvne eiceko atekat ecke-mele em mvhakv cuko atehke tetayet omvres, momen mvhakv cuko enkapvkekot oh hafastv emeleevn apoken emvculkv ohrolope pale hokkolen hvmkontvlakat oricaket omvres enokketvt munkat ensehoketv herekat omeciceen esossicet omhoyekon omat; momis ecke melet ohrolope palen hakkolohkakat hoyvneciеet ont omet eneuko emvtotketv afvstvr' heret emocet on omat meske etektvnkof eneuko ayepe tetayet omvres; momen ecke melet vfastvn ocet omen mv vfastvt cokv heckv euko rakrakat hvmkvteken erlicepe tetayet emetektvnken omat momecepe tetayet omvres.

Sᴇᴛ. 2. Ecke mele em mvhakv euko oh hafastvlke mv mvhakv euko esiyeciekv evtokonawv fiecihocan esaheeet hopoetake emvhonkvtkv esfveken ahakv aevkkvyen apohohyvte emunkvt omvres.

Oh hvkvsamis, Ehole 6, 1893.

LEKVS PELMVN, Mekko.

NUYAKV MVHAKV CUKO.

Sᴇᴛ. 1. *Este Maskoke Tolwv-vlke akerrickv hayat:* Cokv heckv euko oh haketeevlken tulwv-vlket yekeetvn emet emvcahnet os, momat et Nuyakv mvhakv euko ohfvcev este Maskoke Tulwv-vlke momen Ohfeskvlke emeteliketv etepakat etemfveeetv, 1883, etenhayvte ocan etievren, momen mv eticat heyv ohrolope aye erespokofvn omvres.

Oh hakvsamis, Ehole 1, 1893.

LEKVS PELMVN, Mekko.

APUEKV EMVHAKV ESEMMVHERICKV.

Sᴇᴛ. 1. Apuekv aseeyievlke oh feyiev ohrolope hokkolen enwiketv hueret omvres.

SET. 2. Tulwv-vlket in wiketv huericet omvres.

SET. 3. Esehvlvtkv cvtokonawv cukpe-rakko pale hokkolen ($20,000.00) hayet cvtokonap afastvn en wakecet omvres, mohmet ohrolope omvlkvn cvtokonawv estomosen heckuecat tvlwv-vlke nakaftan en kerkuecet omvres.

Oh hakvsamis, Otvwoskv-rakko 19, 1893.

LEKVS PELMVN, Mekko.

ESNESVLK'ESFEYICKV EMVHAKV SEMVHERICKV.

SET. 1. Esnesvlke esfeyickv ahakv hakvte ocat hiyometapvke haket os:

Sahorepueckv wieyvlke, ohrolope arahkv $25.00
Oh huehke wieyvlke, cukot ot munkat escuk'ahak' ofvn on omat, netta arahkv 3.00
Oh huehke wieyvlke, etehoyvnkv vlkan oa omat, netta, arahkv 2.00
Nak' heckv esfullvlk', enrahkv kvckose, nvrkvpuce omosis, estefeyice esfullat, nettv-cakoce arahkv 1.00

Oh hakvsamis, Otv-woskv-rakko 27, 1893.

LEKVS PELMVN, Mekko.

SET. 1. Tulwv-vlke emmekko yekcetv enheckat Estv Cakon apohkv en hahyen pun tvsekiah toko pomekvnv ofv oce cvpkoce ateloye, wieyat esafekhonnicvren kicares.

Oh hakvsamis, Otvwoskv-rakko 25, 1893.

LEKVS PELMVN, Mekko.

EOMEKVLKE OHFVCCV.

SET. 1. Este estomákatet eomekvlket omet cvtokonawv tvleme cvwaket omvres make tulwv-vlke ahakv hayvte ocat hiyomet esemvherickv haket os: Este estomet soletawv ohfvccvn Wacenv encvtokonawvn cvwepet on omat eomekvlke tulwv-vlke cvtokonawv enficcicat celayeko tetayet omvres.

Oh hakvsamis, Otvwoskv-rakko 18, 1893.

LEKVS PELMVN, Mekko.

CORAK' OHKAKV EMONICV OHFVCCV.

SET. 1. Heyv ahakv hahke erenpvlhvmke tonomat ekvntvckv enfvccecv estomet corakohkakv a emonicv paletv, monkat atotkicetv emetektvnkekot omvres; momen fvccecv estomet heyv ahakvn kacen omat enhelvpke ocen mekkot enwiketv ossicet omvres; momen este estomet corak' ohkakv emonicv omen fvccecvt ohmelliyen atotket o estomis tvlwv-vlke enfekekot omvres.

Oh hakvsamis, Ehole 6, 1893.

LEKVS PELMVN, Mekko.

NENE LETKCV OHFVCCV.

SET. 1. Tvlekesvlke pometvlwv ohfvccv nak' emvfastvlket Tulwv Hvtke erasehokvranan hayvraneyvtetot hayeyet on omat hiyomet yekcetv enhecket os. Momen atotkvre emvcahneyet os, momat et, Hayoce ennetta 25, 26, 27, ohrolope 1866, Wacenv enrakrakvt ahakvn hayvtet ocet os, momatet mv ahakvt metke-letkv en nene kerkvken pometvlwv ropoteevren emetektvneeet omatet hvtvm ekvnv akerkv pale hokkole entvptvhe oren metke letkv en nene mestv mi vlkis awakhoken eskerkueheet ohmet, mome eskerkan akerkv hvmke folotke vlken retewarwvke omen eroh hakerriheet omatet. mome retewarkan hvmken nene letkv pucasvken emet, hvmken tohtasket, hvtvm emet, momen ayeceeet erespoyet os. Heyv ahakv hiyome ocan Waceuv enrakrakvt etievren pun tvlekesvlket orosen acehvllvkvres.

Oh hakvsamis, Ehole 6, 1893.

LEKVS PELMVN, Mekko.

TULWV-VLKE EM-MEKKO,

ETEMVRKV OHFVCCV.

Set. 1. Rafo-rakko 5, 1891, atehke ayat este estomet Tulwv-vlke em-mekko haket omekares ahakv acakkvye etemvrkv-rakko hakat tvsekiah sulkat satakat omvlkvn etohkvhlet omhoyan nvrkvpv hoyvnen enhecke saset omekon omat, ahakv impvtakv ofv Mekko hakv ohfvccv ocat faccose ohyvteketv heyvn oket omekv.

Oh hakvsvmkv sekon, Ahakv haket os, 1891.

FVCCECVLKE ENCOKV-HAYVLKE OHFVCCV.

Set. 1. Fvcceev estomet en cokv-hayv eme en nakvftetv-cuko ehomv ahakv haye tetayat emetektvneeekot omvres; momen fvcceev estomet heyv ahakvn kacet on omat enwiketvn ossihocet omvres.

Otowoskv-rakko 26, 1893, Oh hakvsvmkv haket os.

LEKVS PELMVN, Mekko.

AHAKV-HAYV RAKKO EMVHAKV.

Set. 1. Ahakv-hayv ahakv kerre heren, momen este Maskoke emvhakv kerre heren, momen este Hvtke emponvkv momen este Maskoke emponvkau kerren hiyome Tvlwv-vlke nakvfte kakatet enwiketv hayvres, momen emvtotketvt heyvt omvres: este estomen, enwiketvt ot munkot o estomis, Tvlwv-vlket ahueran enhayet munkat emocet on omat, momen mv ahuera nake arahkvn munkat nake ohfvecen haket omvtet o estomis, momen evtokonawv ensulke estomepet o estomis. Fvcecev Hvlwvlke ehomvn opunayecvres, momen yekcen oh hatotkvres; momen opunayeckv ton omat Kaco-hvsse hvmke Fvcecev Hvlwe nakaftof aliceevres. Hiyome Tvlwv-vlke emvhakv-hayv hakat ton omat esehvlvtkvn hayvres evtokonawv eukpe-rokko palen ($10,000.00) mohmet mekkon enwakeevres, momen sehvlvtkv hayat ton omat emvtotketv facose afvstvranan hayet omvres. Tvlwv-vlke mvhakv hayv ton omat yekcetvn ocet omet ekvntvckv fvcecevlke nekeyicet omvres, momen esten feyicvranet Fvcecev Hvlwe ehomvn enfvcecen omat ekvntvckv fvcecevlken oh tohken mvt enfeyicaket omvres, momen este enwiketv huererepat ot munkat enwiketv tokot o estomis Tvlwv-vlket ahuericet omvtet on fekvranen enfvcecen feyiekvn komhoyet on omat ahakv, 1893, esanorihoevte ocat esetenwarke XIII. enrvkpvlke 90 & 91 ahakv ocat anvtteeekot omvres feyickv ohfvecv tat. Tvlwv-vlke emvhakv-hayv emvtotketv atotke are momen hompat tepakat emvhuerv hayat Tvlwv-vlket feket omvres, momen evtokonawv heckuehee Catokonap Afastv ohrvkpalat a ossen evtokonawv hvmkat kvnsatkv hvnmket enhecket omvres. Tulwv-vlke mvhakv-hayv Rafo-rakko 5, 1893, atehke ayat ohrolope hokkolen huervres. Ohrolope omvlkvn Tulwv-vlken eme ohkerkuecet omvres.

Ehole 3, 1893, Oh hakvsvmkv haket os.

LEKVS PELMVN, Mekko.

KVMISSVNVLK' TUTCENAT EMVHAKV.

SET. 1. Este tutcenen momvr' tetaye vlken kvmissvnvlken hiyome Tulwv-vlke nakvfte kakatet enwiketvn sehoyvres, momen enwiketv hahoyan apaken emvtotketv aliceevkvres momen esapeyet hvtvm Tulwv-vlke en nakvftetv ohrolope, 1894, omof remeyoksievres. Este tvsekiv toko pometvlwv ofv apokan omvlkvn encoko perievkvres, momen cuko svrahrvkv nacomet atehket on omat enhocefhokvn encvwvkvres, momen emetvlwvt ot hvtvm ena enheckv estomet omat eskerkuecvkvres, momen apuekv nacomen epocasvket ot munkat epocase oket esapoket on omat mvn eskerkuecvres. Momen oh hatvlakat ahopaye mahet omekot o estomis ekvnv enkololuecakat capofv' tot, pastv tot, svtv mvppe rafechoyat tot, cvpofoce tot munkat tvlofv tot on omat cuko hvpo omakis satke nacomen omaket on omat eskerkuecvkvres, momen nake ohhahicakat tis cukot ot, corakko hutet ot, nake remetvkv estomis oh hahice epocase omet o atekat eskerkuecvkvres, momen mome este apokat naket emvtotketvt omen yekcetv estomat emelecvn epocase omet esapoket on omat eskerkuecvkvres.

Momen tvsekiv toko mome apokakat estomet etektvnke enheciken apuekv tot, cvpofv tot, pastv tot munkat remetvkvt o estomis epocase oket esapoket on omat esfackosen eskerkuecvkvres momen hvtvm Tulwv-vlke nakaftof emeohkerkuecvkvres.

SET. 2. Heyv ahakv emvheckv esfackose ayvre ohfvecan este catvke emestv cakon apohkvn enhayeyet os, momatet Kvmissvnvlke esarvrvkvn tvlof' ahecievlke hvmkvlken ahorkvsuecvres momen mv momecat tat nake emafvstetv tis emocof este tis oh hueketvn eyacaken omat ese vnicvkvr' tetayen em momecet omvres. Kvmessvnvlke estomat to estomis oketv momvr tetayet ohcakken omat ekvntvckv estoman atotket aret on omat mv ekvntuckv corakkohkakv atehkan atotkice tetayet omvres, momen corakkohkakat emonievren eyahcet fvccecvn empohen omat fvccecvt apohkv momat emapohicet omvres.

Set. 3. Kvmissvnvlket pun tvsekiah tokot pomekvnvn liken eshecaket omatet etemfvccetv Wacenv entenhayeyvte ocat tot, munkat pomvhakv tis vnrvpen liket on omat estv cakon enkerkucevkvres momen ossievren empohvkvres, momen aketv momvr tetayet oret ont oman estv cakot afekrvkkekot munkat ossiccepekon omat Kvmissvnvlket este cate en Kvmmessvnv en homahtvn enkerkuecvkvres momet ossievren empohvkvres.

Set. 4. Enhomv ahakv hahoyvte ekvntvckv ahakv emonievlket pon tvsekiah toko pomekvnv fullan hocefkokvn encawet estv-cakon enkerkuecaket omvres make ocat vslepet os, momis ahakv emonievlke enfeketv ohrolope arahkv cvtohonawv cukpe humke ($100.00) emoh hatvlaye ocat tat emunkepvres.

Sec. 5. Kvmissvnvlke enfektetv netta arahkv cvtokonawv tutcenet ($3.00) omvres, momen tvlof aheeievt cvtokonawv hvmket ($1.00) omvres, momet o estomis Kvmessvnv hvmkose a emoniev tepakat ohrolope hvmkat cvtokonawv cukpe rakko hvmkat ($1000.00) hoyvnekot enhecket omvres.

Ehole 3, 1893, Oh hakvsvmkv, haket os.

LEKVS PELMVN, Mekko.

EKVN' TEWARKV VNRVPE AKERRICKV.

Set. 1. Este Maskoke tvlwv-vlke heyvt emvkerrickvt

os. Este Cate etvlwv cahkepat hiyome esvrvhka ahakv e 'enhayepe apokat em mvrahiket ohmen Wacenv ofv ekvn' warkv rakrvke ennakvftetv, emmekko omakis oce eslilakat omet este Maskoke emekvnv aseset yvmvn haket on omat este Maskoke tvlwv-vlke en tvsekiv evkkvk' sekat kakat emenak' oekv atekat emvyvmahket omvranet omes, monkv Wacenv-tvlwv-vlket mome nake emvrahkvre, monkat Oklvhomvn a vlveeyvre ohfveev, akerriekv epoh hayet apohkvn, pun wakecet on omat nake hereko heret ont os komvraneyet omes momen estohmomosen vnrvpeye tetayet on omat momeevraneyet omes.

Set. 2. Wacenv tvlwv-vlke espoke nakaftvnke omof ahakv hayvnke aevkkvyen kvmessvnvlke monkat kvmittvlke omis atothoyen omat tvlwv-vlke Em-mekkot heyv akerriekvn enwakeevres, momen hvtvm este cate en kvmessvnv en homahtv momen pomestv cako tepakvn emvtotvres.

Ehole 1, 1893, Oh hahvsvmkv haket os.

LEKVS PELMVN, Mekko.

$600,000.00 FIYECICAT.

Set. 1. Oklvhomv ekvnv wihoye evtokonawv cukpe rakko acule hokkole ($2,000,000.00) heckvte likat a osset evtokonawv cukpe rakko cukpe epaket ($600,000.00) osiyen este Maskoke tvsekvyvt ekv feketvn ete wahlvres.

Set. 1. Hiyome tvlwv-vlke nakvfte kakat lapeceet ahakv esen hahicet ohmen mv aevkkvyen evtokonawv ossicaranet os.

Atowoskv-rakko 25, 1893, Oh hahvsvmkv haket os.

LEKVS PELMVN, Mekko.

$600,000.00 APOHETV OHFVCCV.

Set. 1. Tvlwv-vlke em-mekko yekcetv enhecket os momen acahnetv enhaket os, momatet ohrolope 1866 omof ekvnv Wacenv emeyvte ocat, momen hvtvm Rafo-cose 19. 1889, omof mv ekvnv eta Wacenv ehmeye hvtvm cvtokonawv pon heckvte likan a ossen cvtokonawv cupke rakko epaken Wacenv enrakrakv cvtokonawv empohetv ohfvccv ahakv hayvte ocat acvkkvyen empohvres, momet mv apohat pon cvttoknap afastv a enfehokvren apohet omvres; momen hiyome apohkv hakat Tvlwv-vlke enyekce eteropottet omvres.

Ohole 4, 1893, Oh hakvsvmkv haket os.

GEN'L L. W. COLBY, PVLLETV OHFVCCV.

Set. 1. L. W. Colby, ahakv-hayv hofonne huervte, Tvlwv-Hvtke liken, este Maskoke tvlwv-vlke emvhakv-hayvn paleyet os, momatet pon tvsekiah Wacenv entvsekiah nake enyvmahkvte maketv ocan momen Wacenv emvhuera oponayeckv nakvftetv cuko likat ot momen Wacenv enfaceeckv hvlwe ehomv tis opunvkv epohkawvphoye ocan opunayecvranet os, momen nake mv omat etat hvtvm epohkvwvpkvranvtet ot momet on omat pomvfvstvranet os: momen ohrolope tuteenen huervranet os, momen ohrolope arahkv cvtokonawv cukperakko ostet enhecket omvres.

Set. 2. Ahakv-hayv hiyome palleyat Tvlwv-vlke emmekkot etemfvccetv hotcen hayet etemfvccvres.

Set. 3. Ahakv-hayv sen feketv cvtokonawv fieket os, momon esfeketv cvtokonap escaekvn mekkot sossievres, momen cvtokonap afastvt pon tvleme a ossen cutokonap escaekv ohfekvres, ahakv en mak maketv vcvkkvyen.

Ehole 6, 1892, Oh hakvsvmkv haket os.

EKVN' SATKV WAKECETV OHFVCCV.

Set. 1. Este maskoke Tulwv-vlke akerrickv hayat:—Este hokkole, akerrvkeko, momen maskoke kvntvckv Ufalv kvntvckv tepakat kakvkekon, mekkot oh mellvres, momen mv ekvnwarkv hokkolat emetenrvwv ekvnsatkvn wakeevkvres, momen Hopoeth Yaholv en wakv huten aliceheet esahoyet Tvklik' Vpakv Uekiwv kihoce ocakan eresorhoyvres, momen cokelen evkevheeet ekvn' satkv eskerkv hayvkvres, momen Cokotv etvlofv ekvn' satkv estvmin liket on omat eskerkue-evkvres, momen hiyome Tvlwv-vlke nakvfte kakan emeohkerkueevkvres.

Otowoskv-Rakko 14, 1893, Oh hakvsvmkv haket os.

EKVN' SATKV OH HAKVSVMKV.

Set. 1. Akerrickv Tvlwv-vlke hayvte acvkkvye Sesv Laevs Mase Haeo tepake oh melhohye Maskoke Kvn' tvckv momen Ufalv Kvn' tvckv eme tenrvwv, W. E. Gentry & Co. en neskv cuko enhonerv estele ahopakv cukpe hokkolen pale hokkolen momen Fisher Mercantile Co. en neskv cuko enhonerv estele ahopakv cukpe hvmken pale oste tuteenohkake ekvn' satkv wakeevkvte ocan Tvlwv-vlke e'enakuecet os, momen mvt ekvn satkv fveeat omvres maket os.

Otowoskv Rakko 24, 1893, Oh hakvsvmkv haket os.

ESTE OPUNAYEHOCAT EMENAK OCKV ENHALVTETV.

Set. 1. Heyv ahakv hoyahne ayat atekat ekvntvckv

fvcceckv eukot ot monkat fvccceckv hvlwe ehomvt o estomis este opunayeckv oh hahoye hueratet emenak ockvn wieyvranet, monkat pometvlwv ertopvrvn akueyvranet omen estoponayece hueratet kerren omat, momen mv wiye monkat akueyatet oh faccet on omat emv huerv fekekare esvrahkvn on omat, estoponayece hueratet fvcceevn apohkvn en haye tetayet omvres opunaye hoce hueratet eme nak ockvn wiye karen monkat akueyekaren.

Sᴇᴛ. 2. Momis fvcceev yekcetv ossiceko emunken estoponayece hueratet akerrvlke hokkolat esen nacomekon esehapvyet enke kvwvpkv eteropotten nake opunayehoce ocaten wihoyaranet os monkat akuehoyvranet os maket kerkueevres, momet nake estemoponayece ocat enrahkv etepvkocken a en sehokvlke heraken hokkolat sen nacomekon ocet esehvlvtkv hayet omvres, momen sehvlvtkv hayat estoponayecatet fvccekon okvteton vnrvpet fvcciyet ohmen nake esten halatvte omecicen naket yvmahkvten omat esfeketv esarahkvt omvres.

Sᴇᴛ. 3. Este oponayehoce hueratet nake emoponayehoce ocaten fvcceev eteropotten enhvlvthoyet ont omaten wieyet monkat etvlwv ertopvrvn akueyet on omat horkopv omen oh hakerrihocvres, momen horkopkv emahakvn esafvshotvres.

Ehole 6, 1893, Oh hakvsvmkv haket os.

AHAKV EMPVTAKV MOCVSSE HAYETV OHFVCCV.

Sᴇᴛ. 1. Este Maskoke entasekiah este honvntake emvculkv oricakat atekat emetvlwoce ofv estvmvn en nakvftetvn hayvket omaken omat Rafo Rakko ennettv 15, 1893, omof mvn etoh nakvftvres, mohmen eme tvlwoce esarvhkv tvlekesvlke hokkolen oh hetemaret enwiketvn hayvkvres, momen tvlekesvlke hiyome hakakatet Rafo-Cose Tuste en hateceskv omof Okmvlken nakvftvres, mohmet tvlekesvlke hvmkvteken ohliketv ohlikvn hiyvkvres momen cokv-hayv yvtekv tepakat vnrvwv sehoken hayvkvres.

SET. 2. Tvlekesvlke hiyome e' etetakuecakof momosen Este Maskoke tvlwv-vlke oh fvcevn Ahak.. empatakv moevssen etetakuecvkvres, momen etetakuecakof mekkon enwakecv-kvres.

SET. 3. Ahakv empvtakv mocassat mekkon enwakkof mekkot estatohtet ohmen ahericet este Maskoke emponvkvn etohtvlhuehoevres mohmet este Hvtke emponvkv este Cate emponvkv tempvlsen esanorihoevres, mohmen cokv hvmkvlken etvlwoce em mekkvken esarahrvkvn mekkot ohtotvres, mohmet tvlwv mekkvken mekkot enkerkuecet omatet emetvlwv tvsekiah etemvrkv vnice tetayat atekat nakvfvteevkvren kievres mohmet nakvfteeakof ahakv empvtake moevsan enwakeevkvres momen e 'enakueevkvranat hvtvm monkat ohfvcevn oh hetemvrvkvres. Etvl' arahkv ahakv empvtakv oh hetemvrakat Kaco-hvsse Tuste esahokkolan etemvraket omvkvres.

Setemvrkv cokv mekkot etetakueeevres, mohmen etempvlsen eskerkuecet omhoyvres momen hvmkaten tvlwoce em mekkot afekhonicet omvres momen hvmkaten mekkvke emohliketv oh likvn ematothoyvres, mohnen ohrolope 1894 Tvlwv-vlke nakaftof mekkvlke emohliketv ohlikvt etemvrkv cokv omvlkvn Tvlwv-vlken en wakeevres.

SET. 4. Ahakv empvtakv moevse hahoyan tvsekiah sulkat ennarkvpv hoyvnet oh hakvsvmet oh hetemaret on omat mekkot oh kerkuecet oponvkvn estvlemievres, momofvn este Maskoke tvlwv-vlke em mvhakv-empvtakvn haket omvres, momet o estomis, ahakv empvtakv hiyome ocat ot momen mv emeleev ahokoce ocakat tis momen este enwiketv hiyome sapaklat o estomis estomen esahopvnet omekares hiyome mekketv hvmkat oketv respoket omekot o atekat, momis hvtvm etemvrkv-rakko hakat ahakv empvtakv moevs-sat aevkkvyen etemvrkv haket omvres.

SET. 5. Tvlekesvlke nakvfte kake etekat netta arahkv evtokonawv hokkolet en heeket omvres momen nakvftetv apeye hvtvm yefoleeat akerkv arahkv narkvpocet en heckaket omvres.

SET. 6. Heyv ahakv aevkkvye tvlekesvlke nafaftat netta eakoee esapakekat netta pale hokkolat hoyvnekon nafaftet omvres.

SET. 7. Heyv ahakv sayeeickv ohfveevn evtokonawv eukpe rakko eahkepet (5,000.00) fieket os, momen omvlkekot o estomis etetayen omat mv atekoset yamahket omvres.

Ehole 1, 1893, Oh hakvsvmkv haket os.

AHAKV.

ENHOMV OCVTE OHFVCCV.

FVCCECV HVLWE FVCCECVTE.

NAK' AHOSKE OHFVCCV.

Lekvs Pelmvn, Mekko:

Ahakv ohrolope 1893 sanorihoevte, rvkpvlkv 94, esetenwarke 267 oeat ohfveev apohkv ponhayetsket os. Mv ahakv hiyomet os, "Hopoetaken oevket on omat hopoewv enheekat etapometat enheeket omvres." maket os, momen apohkv hayetskat heyvt os, "honvnwvt ot monkat hokte tis ehlet ohmen, nak' ahoske afvshoteko emonken hvtvm hvmkat elen omat, espoke elat enhomv elat emenak oekv enkvpihoce tetayet omehaks?"

Akerriekv aheriect oh hayeyat heyat os: Honvnwv tis eles, monkat hokte tis eles, momen nak ahoske afvshoteko emonken hvtvm hvmkat eles, momet on omat espoke elat enhomv elvte emenak oekv enheeke tetayet os hesake huere enheeke tetayat etvpometat.

ESPAHEHCV,

Akocoknose Ohliketv Ohlikv.

Ehole 3, 1893.

ETEHVLVTKV OHFVCCV.

Lekvs Pelmvn, Mekko:

Apohkv hiyomen pon hayecket os: "Estet etehalatet omatet etemfveeetv eten hayet hoteen hayet monkat akerrvlke hokkolat oren ocet etemfaecet omen, akerrvlket ensataken omat ahakv aevkkvyet omvres" make ahakv ocat ohyvtekeyvren pon pohetsket os.

Akerrickv hayeyat heyvt os:

Etehvlvtkv ahakv aevkkvyet omekot omes etemfveeetv hakat hoteet omekot omen akerrvlke hokkolet satvket omekot o etekat, momen estet etehvlvtvranet on omat etemfveeetv hoteen hayahket ohmet ahakv aevkkvyen etensataket omekot o atekat fveeeevtat monkat erkenvkv tis etehalvtepueeeko tetayet os.

ESPAHEHCV,

Akocoknose Ohliketv Ohlikv.

Ehole 3, 1893.

ENHOMV AHAKV OHFVCCV.

OHROLOPE 1893 SANORIHOCVTE.

Setenwarke lopotskosat 324 hiyomet omvranet omvtes: "Corakkohkakv en kapetvnet apuek' somkv enkerkuehoce atekat omvlkvn estvlemievres hvsse epaken, momet estofvn wiyvranet momet estvmvn wiyvranet omat eskerken omvres, momen oketvt cakkof oh hueket wiyvres, momen esfeketvtat evtokonap escaekv, Co' ekv Ahake monkat evtokonawvn cawet omvres.,"

Setenwarke lopotskosat 329 heyvt oh hvpvkvranet omvtes:

"mohmen apuek' somkv nesaten, momen ohfvccchee enhvlvthoyvten, tekvpvke tutcenat tekvpvke hvmken enfehoket omvres."

Setenwarke lopotskosat 115 heyvt oh hvpvkaranet omvtes: "Momen Kvntvtskv Fvcccev evtokoaawv eukpe rakko hokkolen sehalvtkv hayet omvres.

NENE LETKV OHFVCCV.

SET. 1. Tvlwv-vlke akerrickv hayat: Este Maskoke tvlwv-vlke nakvfte kakat heyvt emvkerrickvt os: Este estomet emetohkvlketv hayet ont omet. Wacenv tvlwv-vlket emetektvnecet ont omen, pomekvn' satkv hvs' ossv fvccv wakkan a etoh walvppiket atet M., K. & T. R. R. Kihoce nene-letkv wakkan Maskoke momen Ufalv metenrvwvn yohhalvheet mvn ayokkicet hvmkose hahket wvhvlv fvccv ayen hayessasen omat etemfvccetv Wacenv 1866 etenhayeyvte ocat acvkkvyet omes; mv etemfvcetvt este estomet Wacenv tvlwv-vlket yekcetv emen emetohkvlketvn hahyet ohmen Kvmessvnv enhomahtvt emoh hakvsvmen pomekvn' satkv hvs' ossv fvccv wakkan a etoh walvppiket hvs' vklatkv fvccvn, monkat" wvhvlv fvccv tis ayen hayetayat emetektvnecet os, momen momet haket on omat nene letkv hahoyvre ohfvccv etemfvccetv Wacenv etenhayeyvte eteropotte etektvnke estemeyvte esohfveket omvres: momet o estomis este emetohkvlketv estoman Wacenet emetektvnecet omvres maketvtan makekot os.

Ehole 3, 1893, Ohhakvsvmkv haket os.

FVCCECV HVLWE ENFVCCECKV.

Fvcccev Hvlwe nake fvcceeat emeyoksen ahakv empvtakvt

hayet os, monkv naken Fveeev Hvlwet fveeeevtet ont oman hvtvm opvnayehocet on omat ahakv empvtakv emvheekvn eticet omes.

D. N. McINTOSH.

Etoponayeevlke estimi vlkis akerrvt ena hvmket omepet o estomis nake kerkueeat fveeeckv euko estomis ehomv e enakuehocet omvres, momen nake opunayeekv oeat ohfveee-eeheret omekot o estomis mv a alveee heret omet o etekat e enakuehocet omvres.

JAMES FIFE.

Ahakv Cokv-rakke ohrolope 1893 esanarihoevte oeat hiyomet esem maheriket os: Tvsekiah hahoyvte e hoeefhokv oeat Lizzie Hawkins, Josephine Bruner momen M. O. Rickets make oeat aslet os momen ayoposket hiyomet omvranet os:

Thomas Hawkins, Josephine Bruner momen M. A. Rickets.